FLYING INTO CHRISTMAS

Pop and Fiddle duets for two Violins

Book One

arr. Myanna Harvey

Cover Painting:
Moonbike, Greg Harvey (acrylic on canvas)

CHP439

©2022 by C. Harvey Publications® All Rights Reserved.

www.charveypublications.com - print books & free sheet music blog
www.learnstrings.com - downloadable books & chamber music

FLYING INTO CHRISTMAS
Pop and Fiddle Duets for two Violins, Book One

all duets arranged by Myanna Harvey

Table of Contents

Title	Page
1. **Jingle Bell Rock***	2
2. **Reel on the Housetop**	4
3. **Winter Wonderland***	6
4. **Jingle Bell Jig**	8
5. **The Little Drummer Boy***	10
6. **We Wish You a Hoedown Christmas**	12
7. **Frosty the Snowman***	14
8. **Bell Carol Dance**	16
9. **Have Yourself a Merry Little Christmas***	18
10. **Rock the Halls**	20
11. **Let it Snow! Let it Snow! Let it Snow!***	22
12. **Dance of the Three Kings**	24
13. **Parade of the Tin Soldiers**	26
14. **The Goose is Getting Fat**	28
15. **Dance of the Reed Flutes from *The Nutcracker***	30
16. **Toyland from *Babes in Toyland***	32
17. **March of the Toys from *Babes in Toyland***	34

*Used by permission, listed on each duet page.

Flying Into Christmas for Two Violins, Book One

Jingle Bell Rock

arr. M. Harvey

JINGLE BELL ROCK
Words and Music by JOE BEAL and JIM BOOTHE
Copyright © 1957 (Renewed) CHAPPELL & CO., INC.
This Arrangement © 2022 CHAPPELL & CO., INC.
All Rights Reserved Used by Permission of ALFRED MUSIC
Sole Selling Agent of this 2022 arrangement: C. Harvey Publications®
It is illegal to photocopy or reproduce the music in this book.

Flying Into Christmas for Two Violins, Book One

Reel on the Housetop

Hanby, arr. M. Harvey

©2022 C. Harvey Publications® All Rights Reserved.

Flying Into Christmas for Two Violins, Book One

©2022 C. Harvey Publications® All Rights Reserved.

Winter Wonderland

arr. M. Harvey

WINTER WONDERLAND
Words by DICK SMITH Music by FELIX BERNARD
Copyright © 1934 (Renewed) WC MUSIC CORP.
This Arrangement © 2022 WC MUSIC CORP.
All Rights Reserved   Used by Permission of ALFRED MUSIC
Sole Selling Agent of this 2022 arrangement: C. Harvey Publications®

Flying Into Christmas for Two Violins, Book One

Jingle Bell Jig

Pierpont, arr. M. Harvey

©2022 C. Harvey Publications® All Rights Reserved.

Flying Into Christmas for Two Violins, Book One

The Little Drummer Boy

arr. M. Harvey

THE LITTLE DRUMMER BOY
Words and Music by KATHERINE DAVIS, HENRY ONORATI and HARRY SIMEONE
Copyright © 1958 (Renewed) EMI MILLS MUSIC, INC. and INTERNATIONAL KORWIN CORP.
Exclusive Worldwide Print Rights Administered by ALFRED MUSIC
This Arrangement © 2022 EMI MILLS MUSIC, INC. and INTERNATIONAL KORWIN CORP.
All Rights Reserved Used by Permission of ALFRED MUSIC
Sole Selling Agent of this 2022 arrangement: C. Harvey Publications®

Flying Into Christmas for Two Violins, Book One

11

This Arrangement © 2022 EMI MILLS MUSIC, INC. and INTERNATIONAL KORWIN CORP.

We Wish You a Hoedown Christmas

Trad., arr. M. Harvey

©2022 C. Harvey Publications® All Rights Reserved.

Flying Into Christmas for Two Violins, Book One

Frosty the Snowman

arr. M. Harvey

FROSTY THE SNOWMAN
Words and Music by STEVE NELSON and JACK ROLLINS
Copyright © 1950 (Renewed) CHAPPELL & CO., INC.
This Arrangement © 2022 CHAPPELL & CO., INC.
All Rights Reserved Used by Permission of ALFRED MUSIC
Sole Selling Agent of this 2022 arrangement: C. Harvey Publications®

Flying Into Christmas for Two Violins, Book One

Bell Carol Dance

Leontovych, arr. M. Harvey

©2022 C. Harvey Publications® All Rights Reserved.

Flying Into Christmas for Two Violins, Book One

Have Yourself a Merry Little Christmas

arr. M. Harvey

HAVE YOURSELF A MERRY LITTLE CHRISTMAS
Words and Music by HUGH MARTIN and RALPH BLANE
Copyright © 1943 (Renewed) METRO-GOLDWYN-MAYER INC.
© 1944 (Renewed) EMI FEIST CATALOG INC.
All Rights (Excluding Print) Controlled and Administered by EMI FEIST CATALOG INC.
Exclusive Worldwide Print Rights Controlled and Administered by ALFRED MUSIC
This Arrangement © 2022 EMI FEIST CATALOG INC. All Rights Reserved Used by Permission of ALFRED MUSIC
Sole Selling Agent of this 2022 arrangement: C. Harvey Publications®

Flying Into Christmas for Two Violins, Book One

Rock the Halls

Trad., arr. M. Harvey

Flying Into Christmas for Two Violins, Book One

Let it Snow! Let it Snow! Let it Snow!

arr. M. Harvey

LET IT SNOW! LET IT SNOW! LET IT SNOW!
Words by SAMMY CAHN Music by JULE STYNE
Copyright © 1945 (Renewed) PRODUCERS MUSIC PUBL. CO., INC. and CAHN MUSIC COMPANY
All Rights on Behalf of PRODUCERS MUSIC PUBL. CO., INC. Administered by CHAPPELL & CO., INC.
This Arrangement © 2022 PRODUCERS MUSIC PUBL. CO., INC. and CAHN MUSIC COMPANY
All Rights Reserved Used by Permission of ALFRED MUSIC

Flying Into Christmas for Two Violins, Book One

Dance of the Three Kings

Hopkins, arr. M. Harvey

©2022 C. Harvey Publications® All Rights Reserved.

Flying Into Christmas for Two Violins, Book One

Parade of the Tin Soldiers

Jessel, arr. M. Harvey

Flying Into Christmas for Two Violins, Book One

The Goose is Getting Fat

Trad., arr. M. Harvey

Flying Into Christmas for Two Violins, Book One

©2022 C. Harvey Publications® All Rights Reserved.

Dance of the Reed Flutes from *The Nutcracker*

Tchaikovsky, arr. M. Harvey

Flying Into Christmas for Two Violins, Book One

Toyland from *Babes in Toyland*

Herbert, arr. M. Harvey

March of the Toys from *Babes in Toyland*

Herbert, arr. M. Harvey

Flying Into Christmas for Two Violins, Book One

36

Flying Into Christmas for Two Violins, Book One

©2022 C. Harvey Publications® All Rights Reserved.

You Might Also Like:

Fiddles on the Bandstand: Fun Duets for Two Violins Book One

all duets arranged by Myanna Harvey

Table of Contents

	Title
1.	The Entertainer (Scott Joplin)
2.	Take Me Out to the Ball Game (Albert Von Tilzer)
3.	Yankee Doodle (Traditional)
4.	The Stars and Stripes Forever (John Philip Sousa)
5.	El Jarabe Tapatio; *Mexican Hat Dance* (Traditional)
6.	Overture to *William Tell* (Gioachino Rossini)
7.	America the Beautiful (Samuel A. Ward)
8.	I'm a Yankee Doodle Dandy (George M. Cohan)
9.	Jeanie with the Light Brown Hair (Stephen Foster)
10.	My Country, 'Tis of Thee (Traditional)
11.	Drill, Ye Tarriers, Drill (Charles Connolly)
12.	Maple Leaf Rag (Scott Joplin)
13.	Over There (George M. Cohan)
14.	Simple Gifts (Traditional)
15.	The Washington Post March (John Philip Sousa)
16.	Let Me Call You Sweetheart (Leo Friedman)
17.	The Star Spangled Banner (John Stafford Smith)
18.	Funiculì, Funiculà (Luigi Denza)
19.	You're a Grand Old Flag (George M. Cohan)
20.	Summer, from *The Four Seasons* (Antonio Vivaldi)
21.	Armed Forces Medley (Various)
22.	Pomp and Circumstance March No. 1 (Edward Elgar)
23.	Overture to *The Barber of Seville* (Gioachino Rossini)

CHP367
www.charveypublications.com

Take a journey to a simpler time when lawn chairs and blankets would be out under the stars and music would waft out from under the eaves of the wooden bandstand.

These are the tunes that got our feet moving, made us smile, and brought us together. Now, with these violin duets, you can bring the toe-tapping, exuberant joy to others and remind us all that through highs and lows, music can be something we share to keep our spirits up and build community.

From Scott Joplin to John Philip Sousa, these violin duets will invite you up on the bandstand, out for a gig, or out on your lawn to play your heart out! Know any violists or cellists? You can pick up a copy of the viola or cello book and play with those instruments as well; the violin book is fully compatible with the viola and cello books.

This violin book is mostly in first position, with occasional basic third position.

Also available from www.charveypublications.com: CHP365
The Rieding Violin Concerto in B Minor Practice Edition

Concerto in B Minor - Duet

Concerto by O. Rieding
Duet by M. Harvey

Allegro Moderato

©2020 C. Harvey Publications   All Rights Reserved.